I ♥ MY

SANDWICH TOASTER

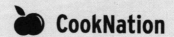 CookNation

I LOVE MY SANDWICH TOASTER
THE ONLY TOASTIE RECIPE BOOK YOU'LL EVER NEED

ISBN 978-1-912155-09-5

DISCLAIMER

CONTENTS

INTRODUCTION

So you love toasties! Who doesn't?

I Love My Sandwich Toaster will banish the notion that toastie fillings are nothing more than a slice of tasteless plastic cheese and cheap ham served in questionable cafés up and down the country.

We aim to bring out the very best in your toastie machine, sandwich grill or panini press. Whether you are a student on a budget, a mum looking for a fast, new and exciting snack for the kids, a professional in need of a great weeknight supper or just someone who wants amazing weekend comfort food – there is toastie here for you to love.

Toasties, made correctly are a fantastic snack, meal or treat any time of the day. Heaven in a sandwich - it's the ultimate comfort food but so much more. They're fun to make, simple and don't cost the earth.

In this easy recipe collection you'll find ideas for all occasions. Our tasty recipes indulge in delicious meat & seafood fillings, meat free choices, sweet & sticky treats and a selection of simple and easy to make homemade extras like chilli jam, chutney, pesto, hummous and coleslaw. For the sake of simplicity we refer to all the sandwiches in our recipes as toasties, however they can all be made equally successfully using a sandwich grill or panini machine.

THE RULES

Rules are made to be broken and our collection of toasties push the boundaries but there are a few basic guidelines you should adhere to:

• Choosing the right bread. Our recipes use different types of bread to mix things up but generally, medium sliced day old bread will achieve the best results – browning nicely and soaking up the ingredients.

- Use good quality cheese.

- Choose something tangy to compliment.

- Ensure you follow the guidelines and instructions for your device as these may differ from the methods and ingredients included in this collection.

TIPS

- Be adventurous. Mix and match. Experiment!

- 'Season' the plates of your sandwich maker or Panini press. This is important as it will ensure your plates remain non-stick. To do this brush the plates lightly with sunflower oil, close the lid and heat to its highest setting for 5 minutes. It is a good idea to do this periodically to get the best out of your machine.

- Always heat up your sandwich maker before adding your sandwich. We recommend the highest setting.

- Invest in a heat-proof pastry brush and a heat-proof non-metallic spatula.

- Always wear oven gloves when using your appliance. The plates obviously become very hot and fingers can easily be burned if you are not careful.

- Either brush your plates or sandwich with oil or butter - our recipes state which.

- Avoid using low fat spreads as these can result in your toastie sticking and

CLEANING

The great thing about toasties is they are generally simple and easy to make with little cleaning up. Here are a few tips to keeping your machine clean after each use.

- Always unplug the machine before cleaning.

- While the plates are still warm but not hot, wipe with damp kitchen towels to remove any grease.

- Use a non-metallic heat-proof spatula to remove more stubborn residue.

- Use a small sponge with warm soapy water to scrub the plates.

- Wipe dry with kitchen paper towels.

- If the plates can be removed for cleaning make sure they have cooled down first.

- No matter how stubborn the mark, never use any abrasive cleaning products or scourers on the plates of your machine. This will ruin the non-stick coating and render your sandwich maker useless. Persevere with warm water and sponges to remove difficult marks.

- Allow the plates to air dry before closing the lid.

ABOUT COOKNATION

CookNation is the leading publisher of innovative and practical recipe books for the modern cook.

With a range of #1 best-selling titles - from the innovative 'Skinny' calorie-counted series, to the 5:2 Diet Recipes collection and I Love My range - CookNation recipe books have something for everyone.

Visit **www.bellmackenzie.com** to browse the full catalogue.

 **CookNation**

MEAT FEAST TOASTIES

CLASSIC HAM AND EGG TOASTIE

INGREDIENTS

- Vegetable or sunflower oil for brushing
- 1 egg
- 1½ tbsp Worcestershire sauce
- ½ tsp Tabasco sauce
- Salt and pepper to taste
- 2 slices bread
- 3 slices cooked ham
- 40g/1½oz Cheddar cheese

METHOD

1 Brush your toastie maker with a little oil to help prevent sticking and make your toastie nice and crispy. Switch on and bring up to its highest temperature.

2 Meanwhile, whisk together the egg, Worcestershire sauce and Tabasco in a bowl. Season with salt and pepper, then pour the mixture into a wide, shallow dish. Soak the bread in the egg mixture.

3 Thinly slice or grate the cheese.

4 Place one slice of egg-soaked bread in the heated toastie maker. Layer the ham and cheese on top. Add the other slice of bread.

5 Close the lid tightly and leave to cook for 3-4 minutes or until the cheese melts and the toastie is crisp and golden.

CHEFS NOTE

Eggs are a great source of protein to give you long-lasting energy.

TURKEY AND PESTO TOASTIE

INGREDIENTS

- Vegetable or sunflower oil for brushing
- 2 slices bread
- 2 tsp basil pesto
- 2 slices cheese
- 2 slices roast turkey

METHOD

1 Brush your toastie maker with a little oil to help prevent sticking and make your toastie nice and crispy. Switch on and bring up to its highest temperature.

2 On one slice of bread, arrange a slice of turkey. Spread one teaspoon of pesto over it. Add the cheese, the rest of the pesto and the second slice of turkey.

3 Top with the remaining slice of bread and place your sandwich in the toastie maker.

4 Close the lid tightly and leave to cook for 3-4 minutes or until the cheese melts and the toastie is crisp and golden brown.

CHEFS NOTE

Serve with a tomato and green leafy salad.

CORNED BEEF TOASTIE

INGREDIENTS

2 slices corned beef
¼ onion
25g/1oz Cheddar cheese
1 tsp mayonnaise
½ tsp mustard
1 tsp sweet pickle relish
2 slices bread
A large knob of butter

METHOD

1 Switch on your toastie maker and bring up to temperature.

2 Shred the corned beef into a bowl. Peel and chop a little onion and add it to the bowl. Grate about an ounce of cheese and add it to the bowl, along with the mayonnaise, mustard, pickle relish, and parsley flakes. Mix it all up.

3 Butter the bread and place one slice in the toastie maker butter side down. Spread the corned beef mixture carefully over the bread. Add the top slice, butter side up.

4 Close the lid tightly and leave to cook for 3-4 minutes or until the toastie is crisp and golden brown.

CHEFS NOTE

Vary the amounts of mayonnaise, mustard and pickle to suit your own taste.

HAM MAYONNAISE TOASTIE

INGREDIENTS

- Vegetable or sunflower oil for brushing
- 2 slices of bread
- 2 tsp mayonnaise
- 40g/1½oz cheese
- 1 slice ham
- 1 slice onion

METHOD

1 Brush your toastie maker with a little oil to help prevent sticking and make your toastie nice and crispy. Switch on your toastie maker and bring up to temperature.

2 While it's heating, grate your cheese and roughly chop the slice of onion.

3 Spread mayonnaise over both slices of bread. Sprinkle half the cheese over one. Add the onion and the ham and then the rest of the cheese. Put the top on the sandwich and transfer to your toastie maker.

4 Close the lid tightly and leave to cook for 3-4 minutes or until the toastie is crisp and golden brown.

CHEFS NOTE

You can use any kind of cheese with this recipe so feel free to experiment with the flavours and quantity.

CHICKEN AND HAM TOASTIE

INGREDIENTS

- 2 slices of bread
- Knob of butter
- 1 tbsp soured cream
- 2 slices Gruyere cheese
- 1 slice cooked chicken breast
- 1 slice ham

METHOD

1 Switch on your toastie maker and bring up to temperature.

2 Meanwhile, slice the cheese, chicken and ham as necessary. Butter one side of each slice of bread; spread soured cream on the other side.

3 Place one slice of bread, butter side down, in the toastie maker. Layer on one slice of cheese, chicken, ham, more cheese, and, finally the second slice of bread, butter side up.

4 Close the lid tightly and leave to cook for 3-4 minutes or until the cheese has melted and the toastie is crisp and golden brown.

CHEFS NOTE

This is a great way to liven up leftover chicken. If you don't have Gruyere cheese just use whatever is to hand.

HAWAIIAN TOASTIE

INGREDIENTS

- 1 ring of tinned pineapple
- Knob of butter
- 2 slices of bread
- 2 slices cheese
- 2 slices cooked ham

METHOD

1 Switch on your toastie maker and bring it up to temperature.

2 While it's heating, open a tin of pineapple and drain; chop one ring into small chunks. Cut 2 slices of cheese.

3 Butter the bread. Place one slice butter side down in your heated toastie maker. Layer on the cheese, ham, and chopped pineapple.

4 Place the remaining slices of bread on top with the butter side up. Close the lid tightly and leave to cook for 3-4 minutes or until the cheese has melted and the toastie is crisp and golden brown.

CHEFS NOTE

Pineapple is great for boosting your vitamin C and energy levels.

BACON AND TOMATO TOASTIE

INGREDIENTS

- 2 slices of bread
- 2 bacon rashers
- 1 tomato
- A few sprigs of flat leaf parsley
- Knob of butter
- Freshly ground black pepper

METHOD

1 Grill the bacon and then roughly chop it.

2 Switch on the toastie maker. While it heats, wash and slice the tomato and chop the parsley.

3 Butter the bread and place the first slice in the toastie maker, butter side down. Arrange the bacon on the bread and sprinkle it with pepper. Place the tomato slices on top, then the parsley, and top with the second slice of bread, butter side up.

4 Close the lid tightly and toast until the sandwich is crisp and golden brown.

CHEFS NOTE

If you don't have parsley, substitute with a couple of lettuce leaves.

PIZZA TOASTIE

INGREDIENTS

- Knob of butter
- 2 slices of bread
- 4 thin slices mozzarella
- 6 slices pepperoni
- 1 spoonful tomato passata

METHOD

1 Switch on the toastie maker. While it heats, cut your slices of mozzarella and pepperoni, and butter the bread.

2 Place one slice of bread in your toastie maker, butter side down. Layer on the mozzarella, pepperoni and a slathering of passata. Finish with the remaining slice of bread, butter side up.

3 Close the lid of your toastie maker tightly and toast until the cheese in melting and sandwich is crisp and golden brown.

CHEFS NOTE
Substitute ketchup for passata if you like.

SAUSAGE, CHEESE AND TOMATO TOASTIE

INGREDIENTS

- 2 sausages
- 40g/1½oz cheese
- 1 tomato
- 2 slices of bread
- Knob of butter

METHOD

1 Grill the sausages, then cut them in half length-wise.

2 Switch on the toastie maker. While it heats, grate the cheese, wash and slice the tomato.

3 Butter the bread and place the first slice in the toastie maker, butter side down. Arrange the sausages on the bread and sprinkle the cheese over them. Place the tomato slices on top, and cover with the second slice of bread, butter side up.

4 Close the lid tightly and cook until the cheese is melted and the toastie is crisp and golden brown.

CHEFS NOTE

If you prefer the Scottish version 1 or 2 slices of square sausage will work just as well.

ROAST BEEF AND ONION TOASTIE

INGREDIENTS

- Pinch salt
- Pinch pepper
- Pinch garlic powder
- 2 tbsp cream cheese
- Knob of butter
- 2 slices of bread
- 2 slices roast beef
- 1 slice onion

METHOD

1 Switch on the toastie maker.

2 While it heats, put the cream cheese in a small bowl and stir in the salt, pepper and garlic powder.

3 Peel and chop a slice of onion. Shred the roast beef.

4 Spread butter on one side of each piece of bread. Spread the cream cheese mixture on the other side.

5 Place one slice of bread, butter side down, in the toastie maker. Add the roast beef and sprinkle with the chopped onion. Place the other slice of bread, butter side up, on the top.

6 Close the lid tightly and cook until the toastie is golden brown and heated through.

CHEFS NOTE

Half a clove of crushed garlic instead of garlic powder is fine too.

CHICKEN AND ROCKET TOASTIE

INGREDIENTS

- Vegetable or sunflower oil for brushing
- 2 slices of grilled chicken breast
- 2 slices bread
- 2 tsp mayonnaise (or to taste)
- 2 tsp Dijon mustard (or to taste)
- 2 slices cheese
- A few rocket leaves

METHOD

1 Use leftover cooked chicken if you have it. If not, grill the chicken breast on both sides until it is cooked through, then remove the chicken to cool and switch off the grill.

2 Brush your toastie maker with a little oil to help prevent sticking and make your toastie nice and crispy. Switch on the machine and bring it up to temperature.

3 Meanwhile, spread a thin layer of mayonnaise and mustard on each slice of bread. Cut a couple of slices of cheese, and rinse a few rocket leaves.

4 Place a slice of cheese on one piece of bread. Add the chicken and rocket, and then the other slice of cheese. Top with remaining bread.

5 Transfer your sandwich to the toastie maker. Close the lid tightly and cook until the cheese is melted and the toastie is crisp and golden brown.

CHEFS NOTE

Rocket has striong anti-oxidant health benefits.

BURGER TOASTIE

INGREDIENTS

Vegetable or sunflower oil for brushing
2 slices of bread
1 large burger
2 cheese slices
Ketchup
1 tomato

METHOD

1 Fry or grill the burger until cooked through. Place it on a piece of kitchen roll to drain off any excess fat.

2 Brush your toastie maker with a little oil to help prevent sticking and make your toastie nice and crispy. Switch on the machine and bring up to temperature.

3 Rinse and slice the tomato. Spread some ketchup on both slices of bread. Place one slice in your toastie maker. Add a slice of cheese, with the burger on top. Add the tomato slices and the other slice of cheese. Top with the other slice of bread.

4 Close the lid tightly and cook until the cheese is melted and the toastie is crisp and golden brown.

CHEFS NOTE

If you prefer, substitute mayonnaise, or another burger topping of your choice, for the ketchup.

CHICKEN AND MUSTARD TOASTIE

INGREDIENTS

- Vegetable or sunflower oil for brushing
- 2 slices of bread
- 2 slices roast chicken
- 2 tsp Dijon mustard
- Parmesan cheese
- Salt and Pepper

METHOD

1 Brush your toastie maker with a little oil to help prevent sticking and make your toastie nice and crispy. Switch on the machine and bring up to temperature.

2 Place one slice of bread in your heated toastie maker. Arrange the chicken over the top, season with salt & pepper and spread with mustard. Grate some Parmesan over the top. Cover with the remaining slice of bread.

3 Close the lid tightly and cook until the toastie is crisp and golden brown.

CHEFS NOTE

If you don't have Parmesan, grate some Cheddar instead, or just add a slice of cheese.

SEAFOOD TOASTIES

TUNA AND ROSEMARY TOASTIE

INGREDIENTS

- 1 small tin tuna in olive oil
- 1 slice onion
- 1 sprig rosemary
- Black pepper
- 2 slices cheese
- 2 slices bread
- Knob of butter

METHOD

1 Switch on your toastie maker to pre-heat.

2 Meanwhile, peel and finely chop a slice of onion. Open a tin of tuna and drain. Tip the tuna into a small bowl. Add the onion. Rinse the rosemary, strip off the leaves and chop them. Add them to the tuna with some black pepper, and mix. Cut two large slices of cheese.

3 Butter the bread and place one slice, butter side down, in your toastie maker. Place one slice of cheese on top, then spread on the tuna mixture. Add the second slice of cheese and top with the remaining slice of bread, butter side up.

4 Close the lid of the machine tightly and leave to cook until the toastie is crisp and golden brown.

CHEFS NOTE

You may find half the tuna mixture is enough for one sandwich.

SARDINE AND TOMATO TOASTIE

INGREDIENTS

- 1 tin sardines in BBQ sauce
- 2 slices bread
- Knob of butter
- Black pepper
- 2 slices tomato

METHOD

1 Switch on your toastie maker to pre-heat.

2 Meanwhile, open a tin of sardines. Mash the fish in a small bowl with some black pepper.

3 Rinse and slice a tomato.

4 Butter the bread and place one slice, butter side down, in your toastie maker. Spread the fish on and top with tomato slices.

5 Close the lid of the machine tightly and leave to cook until the toastie is crisp and golden brown.

CHEFS NOTE

Sardines are oily fish that have many health benefits, including boosting your brain focus.

EASY SALMON TOASTIE

INGREDIENTS

- Sunflower oil for brushing
- 2 slices bread
- 2 tsp tomato pasta sauce
- 1 small tin flaked salmon
- Black pepper
- ¼ red pepper
- 30g/1oz mature Cheddar cheese

METHOD

1 Lightly brush your toastie maker with sunflower oil and switch it on to pre-heat.

2 Meanwhile, open a tin of salmon and mash in a small bowl with some black pepper to taste.

3 Rinse, core and chop the red pepper. Grate the cheese.

4 Smear the sauce on both slices of bread and then spread the salmon on top. Scatter the red pepper over it and then the cheese. Close the sandwich with the second slice of bread and transfer to the toastie machine

5 Close the lid tightly and leave to cook until the toastie is crisp and golden brown.

CHEFS NOTE

Any tinned fish will work with this recipe too, e.g. tuna, pilchards, sardines.

SMOKED MACKEREL TOASTIE

INGREDIENTS

- 1 small smoked mackerel fillet, skinned and flaked
- 2 slices bread
- Knob of butter, for spreading
- 1 tsp English or mild mustard
- 1 tsp creamed horseradish or ketchup
- ½ stalk celery, finely chopped

METHOD

1 Switch on your toastie maker to preheat.

2 Meanwhile, rinse and finely chop the celery. Butter the bread on one side, and smear mustard over the other side.

3 Skin and flake the fish into a bowl and mix with the horseradish and celery.

4 Place one slice of bread, butter side down in the toastie maker. Spread the mackerel mixture over it and add the other slice of bread, butter side up.

5 Close the lid of the machine tightly and cook until the toastie is crisp and golden brown.

CHEFS NOTE

Mackerel is a sustainabe fish you can pick up easily at any supermarket.

SMOKED TROUT TOASTIE

INGREDIENTS

- Sunflower oil for brushing
- 50g/2oz smoked trout slices
- 2 slices of bread
- 2 tsp pesto
- 2 slices cheese
- Salt and ground black pepper

METHOD

1 Lightly brush your toastie maker with sunflower oil and switch it on to pre-heat.

2 Meanwhile, cut the cheese slices.

3 Spread pesto over both slices of bread. Arrange the smoked trout on one slice. Season with salt and pepper. Add the cheese slices and cover with the remaining slice of bread, pesto side down.

4 Close the lid of the machine tightly and cook until the toastie is crisp and golden brown.

CHEFS NOTE

Smoked salmon also works well with this recipe, as does smoked mackerel which is usually cheaper.

FISH FINGER & BAKED BEAN TOASTIE

INGREDIENTS

- 2 slices bread
- Knob of butter
- 3 fish fingers
- 50g/2oz Cheddar cheese
- 5 tsp baked beans

METHOD

1 Grill or fry the fish fingers according to the packet instructions.

2 Switch on your toastie maker to preheat.

3 Grate the cheese and butter the bread on both sides.

4 Place one slice of bread in the preheated toastie machine and layer on the cooked fish fingers, beans and cheese. Top with the remaining slice of bread.

5 Close the lid of the machine tightly and cook until the toastie is crisp and golden brown.

CHEFS NOTE

Baked beans are rich in protein and iron and help keep your energy levels high.

QUICK & EASY TUNA TOASTIE

INGREDIENTS

- Sunflower oil for brushing
- 2 slices bread
- 1 tin tuna
- Handful grated cheese

METHOD

1 Lightly brush your toastie maker with sunflower oil and switch it on to pre-heat.

2 Meanwhile, drain the tuna. Grate a handful of cheese and spread about a third over one slice of bread. Add half the tuna, some more cheese, and then the rest of the tuna. Top with the remaining cheese, and close the sandwich with the second slice of bread.

3 Transfer the sandwich to the toastie machine and close the lid tightly. Cook until the cheese melts and the bread is crispy and golden brown.

CHEFS NOTE

Tuna is a source of complete protein, providing all 10 amino acids your body needs to survive. S

CHILLI TUNA TOASTIE

INGREDIENTS

- Sunflower oil for brushing
- ½ stalk celery
- 1 spring onion
- ½ small chilli
- 1 tin tuna
- 1 tbsp mayonnaise
- Salt
- 2 slices bread
- 2 slices Cheddar cheese

METHOD

1 Lightly brush your toastie maker with sunflower oil and switch it on to pre-heat.

2 Meanwhile, rinse and finely chop the celery, spring onion and chilli (removing the seeds). Drain the tuna and mix it in a bowl with the mayonnaise, celery, spring onion and chilli. Season with salt to taste.

3 Place one slice of bread in the toastie machine. Add a slice of cheese and spread on the tuna mixture. Leave some for another day if it's too much. Top with the other slice of cheese, and the remaining bread.

4 Close the lid of the machine tightly and cook until the cheese melts and the toastie is crisp and golden brown.

CHEFS NOTE

If you don't have spring onions, a slice of red or white onion works too.

PRAWN TOASTIE

INGREDIENTS

- Sunflower oil for brushing
- 2 slices white bread
- 75g/3oz cooked prawns
- 1 tbsp mayonnaise
- Dash of Tabasco sauce or pinch of chilli powder
- Salt and pepper

METHOD

1 Rinse prawns in cold water. Tip them into a bowl.

2 Lightly brush your toastie maker with sunflower oil and switch it on to pre-heat.

3 Mix together the prawns, mayo, Tabasco, salt and pepper.

4 Place one slice of bread in the heated toastie maker. Spread on the prawn mixture and cover with the other slice of bread.

5 Close the lid of the machine tightly and cook until crispy and golden brown.

CHEFS NOTE

Try using Rose Marie sauce in place of mayo if you like.

SANDWICH PASTE TOASTIE

INGREDIENTS

- 1 tbsp cream cheese
- Knob of butter
- 2 slices bread
- 1 tbsp mayonnaise
- ½ tomato finely chopped
- Salt & pepper
- 1 tbsp fish sandwich paste

METHOD

1 Switch on your toastie maker and pre-heat.

2 Mix together the cream cheese, mayo, chopped tomato and fish paste,

3 Butter the bread. Lay one slice, butter side down, in the toastie maker. Spread the fish mixture over it and add the other slice of bread, butter side up.

4 Close the lid of the machine tightly and cook until crispy and golden brown.

CHEFS NOTE

Jars of fish sandwich paste are super cheap and pack a powerful punch in your toasties.

CRAB TOASTIE

INGREDIENTS

- 1 tin crabmeat
- 1 tbsp mayonnaise
- 1 slice of onion, chopped
- 30g/1oz Cheddar cheese
- Black pepper
- ½ tsp mustard
- 2 slices bread
- Knob of butter

METHOD

1 Switch on your toastie maker and pre-heat.

2 Peel and finely chop a slice of onion. Grate the cheese.

3 Open the tin of crab, drain, and tip the crab into a small bowl. Mix in the mayonnaise, onion, cheese, mustard and pepper.

4 Butter the bread and lay one slice, butter side down, in the toastie maker. Spread the crab mixture on the bread – save some for another day if there's too much - and top with the other slice, butter side up.

5 Close the lid of the machine tightly and cook until the cheese melts and the bread is crispy and golden brown.

CHEFS NOTE

If you prefer, use tartar sauce instead of mayonnaise.

VEGGIE TOASTIES

CHEESE, MUSHROOM AND PEPPER TOASTIE

INGREDIENTS

- Knob of butter
- 2 slices bread
- 1 clove garlic
- ½ tomato
- 1 mushroom
- ¼ red pepper
- 4 slices of mature cheese
- Black pepper for seasoning

METHOD

1 Peel & finely chop a clove of garlic. Rinse and slice the tomato, mushroom and pepper. Cut four slices of cheese.

2 Butter the bread and place one slice, butter side down, in the toastie maker. Arrange 2 slices of cheese on top, then the tomato, mushroom and peppers. Sprinkle the garlic over the top along with a little black pepper. Top with the remaining cheese and cover with the second slice of bread.

3 Close the lid tightly and leave to cook for 3-4 minutes or until the cheese melts and the toastie becomes crispy and golden brown.

CHEFS NOTE

If you like, spread some peanut butter on the bread before you build your toastie.

DOUBLE CHEESE AND ONION TOASTIE

INGREDIENTS

- 2 slices bread
- 1 slice onion
- Knob of butter
- Salt to taste
- 2 tsp mayonnaise
- Handful grated Parmesan cheese
- Handful grated mozzarella cheese
- A few leaves of parsley or oregano (if you've got any)

METHOD

1 Switch on your toastie maker to preheat.

2 Rinse and chop the parsley or oregano. Peel and finely chop the onion. Grate the cheese and mix the two types together.

3 In a small bowl, mix the onion, herbs and mayonnaise. Season to taste.

4 Butter the bread and lay one slice, butter side down, in the toastie maker. Sprinkle on half the cheese. Spread the onion and mayonnaise over the top. Add the rest of the cheese and cover with the other slice of bread, butter side up.

5 Close the lid of the toastie maker tightly and leave to cook until the cheese melts and the toastie is crispy and golden brown.

CHEFS NOTE

Just use whatever cheese you have.

CHEESE, TOMATO AND BASIL TOASTIE

INGREDIENTS

- 2 slices bread
- Knob of butter
- 1 slice Cheddar cheese
- ½ tomato
- ½ chilli
- ½ tsp dried basil
- Salt and pepper to taste

METHOD

1 Switch on your toastie maker to preheat.

2 Cut a slice of cheese. Rinse the tomato and chilli. Slice the tomato. Deseed and thinly slice the chilli.

3 Butter the bread and place one slice, butter-side down, in the toastie maker. Layer one slice of cheese, one slice of tomato and a few slices of chilli on top. Sprinkle dried basil and salt and pepper to taste. Cover with the remaining slice of bread, butter-side up.

4 Close the lid of the toastie maker tightly and leave to cook until the cheese melts and the toastie is crispy and golden brown.

CHEFS NOTE

If you have fresh basil, use a few chopped leaves instead of dried.

LEEK AND CHEESE TOASTIE

INGREDIENTS

- 1 leek
- 2 slices tomato
- 2 slices bread
- Knob of butter
- 50g/2oz Cheddar cheese
- 2 tbsp mayonnaise

METHOD

1 Switch on your toastie maker to preheat.

2 Rinse and chop the white part of the leek lengthways into thin strips. Wash and slice the tomato. Grate the cheese.

3 Butter the bread. Place one slice, butter side down, in the toastie maker. Cover with the leeks, half of the cheese, the tomato slices, then the remaining cheese.

4 Spread the mayonnaise on the unbuttered side of the other slice of bread and lay on the sandwich, butter side up.

5 Close the lid of the toastie maker tightly and leave to cook until the cheese melts and the toastie is crispy and golden brown.

CHEFS NOTE

Leeks are rich in vitamins A and K, and are great for all round health.

VEGGIE SAUSAGE AND PEPPER TOASTIE

INGREDIENTS

- 2 vegetarian sausages
- ½ red or yellow pepper
- Sunflower oil for brushing
- 50g/2oz cheese
- 2 slices of bread

METHOD

1 Grill the sausages and pepper, turning frequently. (Brush the pepper with a little oil and some salt beforehand).

2 Brush your toastie maker with a little sunflower oil to help prevent sticking and to make your toastie nice and crisp. Switch it on to pre-heat.

3 Thinly slice the sausage. Chop half the pepper into chunks. Slice or grate the cheese.

4 Place one slice of bread in the heated toastie maker. Cover with half the cheese. Add the sausage and pepper and the rest of the cheese, then top with the other slice of bread.

5 Close the lid of the toastie maker tightly and cook until the cheese melts and the bread is crispy and golden brown.

CHEFS NOTE

Veggie sausages are a good source of protein.

BUTTERNUT SQUASH AND BASIL TOASTIE

INGREDIENTS

- 100g/3½oz roasted butternut squash
- Handful fresh basil leaves
- Salt and pepper
- 50g/2oz cheese
- 2 slices bread
- A little sunflower oil for brushing

METHOD

1 In a bowl, mash the cooked butternut squash. Chop the basil leaves and stir into the squash. Grate the cheese and add to the bowl with salt and pepper to taste.

2 Brush your toastie maker with a little sunflower oil to help prevent sticking and to make your toastie nice and crisp. Switch it on to pre-heat.

3 Spread the squash mixture onto one slice of bread and cover with the other.

4 Transfer the sandwich to the heated toastie maker. Close the lid tightly and cook until the cheese melts and the bread is crispy and golden brown.

CHEFS NOTE

The butternut squash is jam-packed with nutrients, including vitamin B6 which is good for the brain and nervous system.

PEPPER AND SPINACH TOASTIE

INGREDIENTS

- 2 slices bread
- Knob of butter
- 1 tomato
- 50g/2oz cheese
- 2 slices red or yellow pepper
- Handful baby spinach
- Pinch black pepper

METHOD

1 Switch on your toastie maker to pre-heat.

2 Rinse and thinly slice the tomato and pepper. Wash and chop the spinach leaves. Grate the cheese.

3 Butter the bread. Put one slice, butter side down, in the toastie maker. Cover with half the cheese, and arrange the pepper, spinach and tomato on top. Sprinkle with a little black pepper and add the rest of the cheese. Cover with the other slice of bread, butter side up.

4 Close the lid of the toastie maker tightly and cook until the cheese melts and the bread is crispy and golden brown.

CHEFS NOTE

Spinach is a superfood, rich in antioxidants and nutrients essential for a healthy brain and body.

KIDNEY BEAN & SALSA TOASTIE

INGREDIENTS

- ½ red or yellow pepper
- 2 tbsp tinned kidney beans
- 1-2 tsp salsa
- 2 slices bread
- Knob of butter
- 50g/2oz cheese

METHOD

1 Switch on your toastie maker to pre-heat.

2 Meanwhile, tip the beans into a bowl with the salsa and mash them together. Thinly slice or grate the cheese.

3 Butter the bread and place one slice, butter side down, in the toastie maker. Arrange the cheese and mashed beans on the bread. Cover with the remaining slice of bread, butter side up.

4 Close the lid of the toastie maker tightly and cook until the cheese melts and the bread is crispy and golden brown.

CHEFS NOTE

If you prefer a bit more texture, leave some of the kidney beans whole while you mash the rest.

AVOCADO, TOMATO AND PEPPER TOASTIE

INGREDIENTS

- ½ tomato
- ½ red or yellow pepper
- ½ ripe avocado
- Knob of butter
- 2 slices of bread
- Dash of olive oil (optional)
- Black pepper

METHOD

1 Switch on your toastie maker to pre-heat.

2 Meanwhile, rinse and slice the tomato and pepper. Peel, stone and slice the avocado.

3 Butter both sides of the bread. Place one slice in the toastie maker and layer on the slices of avocado, tomato & pepper and drizzle a tiny amount of olive oil over the top. Season and top with the other slice of bread.

4 Close the lid of the toastie maker tightly and cook until the bread is crispy and golden brown.

CHEFS NOTE

Avocados are another superfood, and high in antioxidants that are important for eye health.

SWEETCORN AND CHILLI TOASTIE

INGREDIENTS

- Sunflower oil for brushing
- 2 slices bread
- 1 tbsp tinned sweetcorn
- ¼ green pepper
- ½ green chilli
- 50g/2oz cheese
- Black pepper

METHOD

1 Brush your toastie maker with a little sunflower oil to prevent sticking and help make your toastie nice and crisp.

2 Open a tin of sweetcorn and drain. Put a tablespoonful in a bowl. Rinse and finely chop the green pepper and the chilli (removing the seeds from the chilli). Add them to the bowl. Grate the cheese and throw that in too. Season with black pepper and mix them together.

3 Lay one slice of bread in the toastie maker. Spread on the sweetcorn mixture and cover with the other slice of bread.

4 Close the lid of the toastie maker tightly and cook until the cheese melts and the bread is crispy and golden brown.

CHEFS NOTE

You can use frozen sweetcorn too; just boil it for a minute or two first.

LEFTOVER VEGGIE TOASTIE

INGREDIENTS

- Handful of mixed, cooked vegetables (e.g., carrots, green beans, broccoli, cauliflower, or anything you have leftover)
- 1 tbsp mayonnaise
- Salt and pepper
- Knob of butter
- 2 slices bread
- ½ tomato

METHOD

1 Switch on your toastie maker to pre-heat.

2 Meanwhile, mash the vegetables with the mayonnaise and season with salt and pepper. Rinse and slice the tomato.

3 Butter the bread, and place one slice in the toastie maker, butter side down. Spread the veggie mixture on the bread and top with the tomato slices. Cover with the remaining slice of bread, butter side up.

4 Close the lid of the toastie maker tightly and cook until the cheese melts and the bread is crispy and golden brown.

CHEFS NOTE

Use ketchup instead of mayonnaise if you prefer.

HOT BEAN TOASTIE

INGREDIENTS

- Sunflower oil for brushing
- ½ sweet potato, cooked
- Pinch Cayenne pepper
- 25g/1oz cheese, grated
- 1 tbsp tinned mixed beans
- A few lettuce leaves
- 2 tsp mayonnaise
- 2 slices bread

METHOD

1 Brush your toastie maker with a little sunflower oil to prevent sticking and make your toastie nice and crisp. Switch it on to pre-heat.

2 Meanwhile, mash the sweet potato in a bowl with the cheese and Cayenne pepper.

3 Butter the bread, and place one slice in the toastie maker. Spread the potato mixture on the bread. Add the lettuce on top, then the beans and the mayonnaise. Cover with the remaining slice of bread.

4 Close the lid of the toastie maker tightly and cook until the bread is crispy and golden brown.

CHEFS NOTE

Just drop the sweet potato if you don't have any.

APPLE AND CHEESE TOASTIE

INGREDIENTS

- 1 apple
- 1 handful of grated cheese
- 2 slices of bread
- Knob of butter
- Pinch of ground cinnamon

METHOD

1 Switch on your toastie maker to pre-heat.

2 Peel , core and slice the apple. Grate the cheese.

3 Butter the bread and place one in the heated toastie maker, butter side down. Scatter half the cheese on the bread and arrange the apple slices on top. Sprinkle with cinnamon, add the rest of the cheese and cover with the other slice of bread, butter side up.

4 Close the lid of the toastie maker tightly and cook until the cheese melts and the bread is crispy and golden brown.

CHEFS NOTE

Cheese contains a host of vital nutrients, including calcium which is important for healthy bones and well being.

AROUND THE
WORLD TOASTIES

BASIC AMERICAN CHEESE TOASTIE

INGREDIENTS

- 2 slices bread
- Knob of butter
- 1 white processed cheese slice
- 1 yellow processed cheese slice
- 2 tsp American mustard

METHOD

1 Switch on your toastie maker to pre-heat.

2 Meanwhile, butter the bread. On the unbuttered side spread the mustard on one slice. Layer the white and yellow cheese slices. Top with the second slice of bread, butter side up.

3 Transfer the sandwich to the heated toastie maker. Close the lid tightly and leave to cook until the cheese is melted and the bread is crispy and golden brown.

CHEFS NOTE

Enjoy with a dollop of American sauce!

MEXICAN GUACAMOLE TOASTIE

INGREDIENTS

- Sunflower oil for brushing
- 2 slices white bread
- 1 tbsp guacamole
- Handful grated cheese
- Pinch chilli powder or chopped chilli

METHOD

1 Brush your toastie maker with a little sunflower oil to help prevent sticking and make your toastie nice and crispy. Switch it on to pre-heat.

2 Meanwhile, grate a handful of cheese. Spread a tablespoon of guacamole on one slice of bread and top with the grated cheese and chilli.

3 Transfer the sandwich to the heated toastie maker. Close the lid tightly and leave to cook until the cheese is melted and the bread is crispy and golden brown.

CHEFS NOTE

Guacamole is made from avocado tomato and lime juice, so is high in vitamin C and good for your brain, energy levels and general health!

SWISS CHEESE TOASTIE

INGREDIENTS

- Knob of butter
- 1 garlic clove
- 2 slices bread
- 50g/2oz Emmental cheese
- 1 slice ham
- 2 cornichons sliced lengthwise

METHOD

1 Switch on your toastie maker to pre-heat.

2 Soften the butter and crush a garlic clove into it, mashing to make garlic butter.

3 Cut 2 slices of cheese. Slice two cornichons lengthwise.

4 Spread the garlic butter on the bread. Place one slice, butter side down, in the toastie maker. Place 1 slice of the cheese on top, add the ham and the cornichons and the remaining cheese. Top with the second slice of bread, garlic butter side up.

5 Close the lid of the toastie machine tightly and cook until the cheese is melted and the bread is crispy and golden brown.

CHEFS NOTE

Use any other pickled gherkins you've got it doesn't need to be cornichons.

CURRIED EGG TOASTIE

INGREDIENTS

- 2 eggs
- Sunflower oil for brushing
- 2 tsp mayonnaise
- 1 tsp curry powder
- Salt and pepper
- 2 slices bread

METHOD

1 Hard boil the eggs (around 8 minutes). Rinse them under cold water to cool and peel off the shells. Drop the peeled eggs in a bowl.

2 Brush your toastie maker with a little sunflower oil to help prevent sticking and make your toastie nice and crispy. Switch it on to pre-heat.

3 Meanwhile, mash the eggs with a fork. Mix in the mayonnaise and curry powder. Season to taste with salt and pepper.

4 Place one slice of bread in the heated toastie maker. Spread on the egg mixture and top with the other slice of bread.

5 Close the lid of the toastie machine tightly and cook until the toastie is crispy and golden brown.

CHEFS NOTE

Use mild or hot curry powder – whichever you prefer.

ITALIAN SALAMI AND CHEESE TOASTIE

INGREDIENTS

- 4 slices Italian salami
- 3 slices Italian cheese
- 2 slices bread
- Knob of butter

METHOD

1 Switch on your toastie maker to pre-heat.

2 Meanwhile, dice the salami and cheese slices, and butter the bread.

3 When the toastie maker is up to temperature, place one slice of bread, butter side down, in the machine. Evenly scatter the salami and cheese across the bread, and top with the other slice of bread, butter side up.

4 Close the lid of the toastie machine tightly and cook until the cheese is melted and the toastie is crispy and golden brown.

CHEFS NOTE

Provolone is a lovely Italian cheese but use whatever you have to hand.

SPICY SPANISH CHEESE TOASTIE

INGREDIENTS

- ½ tomato
- ¼ red onion
- 50g/2oz Manchego cheese
- Pinch chilli powder
- 2 slices bread
- Knob of butter

METHOD

1 Switch on your toastie maker to pre-heat.

2 Meanwhile, rinse and finely chop the tomato. Peel and finely chop the onion. Grate the cheese. Combine everything in a bowl.

3 Butter the bread. Lay one slice, butter side down, in the toastie maker. Spread on the cheese mixture and cover with the remaining slice of bread, butter side up.

4 Close the lid of the toastie machine tightly and cook until the cheese is melted and the toastie is crispy and golden brown.

CHEFS NOTE

If you can't get Manchego, use half Parmesan and half Cheddar – less Spanish but still tasty!

FRENCH ONION TOASTIE

INGREDIENTS

- Knob of butter
- ½ tbsp olive oil
- 1 onion
- Salt and freshly cracked black pepper
- 1 tsp fresh thyme
- 2 slices French Gruyère cheese
- 2 slices bread
- Salted butter, softened

METHOD

1 Heat the butter and olive oil in a frying pan. Peel and slice the onion and throw it in the pan. Cook on a low heat and sauté for about 10 minutes. Meanwhile, rinse and finely chop the thyme. Add it to the onions and season with salt and pepper. Cook for another 5 minutes. Remove from the heat and set aside.

2 Brush your toastie maker with a little sunflower oil to help prevent sticking and make your toastie nice and crisp. Switch it on to pre-heat.

3 Meanwhile, lay a slice of cheese on one slice of bread. Spread the onions over it, add the other slice of cheese and cover with the remaining slice of bread.

4 Transfer the sandwich to the heated toastie machine. Close the lid tightly and cook until the cheese is melted and the toastie is crisp and golden brown.

CHEFS NOTE

Try a splash of sherry or brandy to the onions as you cook them.

PEANUT BUTTER, JELLY & BANANA TOASTIE

INGREDIENTS

- 2 slices good quality white bread
- Knob of butter
- 1 tbsp peanut butter
- ½ tbsp jam
- ½ banana sliced

METHOD

1 Switch on your toastie maker to pre-heat.

2 Butter the bread, then turn both slices over. Spread peanut butter on the back of one slice, and the jam of your choice on the back of the other.

3 Peel and slice the banana.

4 Place one slice of bread, butter side down, in the toastie maker. Arrange the slices of banana on the top, and cover with the other slice of bread, butter side up.

5 Close the lid of the toastie maker tightly and cook until the bread is crispy and golden brown.

CHEFS NOTE

Try different jams for a variety of flavours!

HALLOUMI AND TOMATO TOASTIE

INGREDIENTS

- 2 slices bread
- Knob of butter
- Few slices of Halloumi cheese
- 1 fresh tomato
- 1 tsp pesto

METHOD

1 Switch on your toastie maker to pre-heat.

2 Cut enough slices of Halloumi to cover a slice of bread. Rinse and slice the tomato.

3 Butter the bread and place one slice in the toastie maker, butter side down. Spread the pesto on the unbuttered side. Arrange the Halloumi slices on top, add the tomato slices and cover with the remaining slice of bread, butter side up.

4 Close the lid of the toastie maker tightly and cook until the cheese melts and the bread is crispy and golden brown.

CHEFS NOTE

Substitute mayonnaise for pesto if you like.

INDIAN CHUTNEY & CHEESE TOASTIE

INGREDIENTS

- Sunflower oil for brushing
- 2 slices bread
- 50g/2oz cheese
- 1 medium tomato
- ¼ small red onion
- 1 tbsp mango chutney

METHOD

1 Brush your toastie maker with a little sunflower oil and switch on to pre-heat.

2 Slice or grate the cheese. Rinse the tomato and slice. Peel and finely slice the onion.

3 Spread the chutney over both pieces of bread. Arrange the cheese, tomato and onion on one of them. Cover with the other piece of bread.

4 Close the lid of the toastie maker tightly and cook until the cheese melts and the bread is crispy and golden brown.

CHEFS NOTE

Add a little spice too if you like.

KOREAN EGG TOASTIE

INGREDIENTS

- 2 eggs
- 1 small carrot
- 1 slice onion
- 1 tbsp sunflower oil, plus more for brushing
- 2 slices bread
- Salt and pepper
- 1 large slice cheese
- 1 slice ham
- ½ tbsp tomato ketchup

METHOD

1 Crack the eggs into a bowl and whisk them.

2 Peel and finely slice the carrot & onion and add to the beaten egg.

3 Heat the oil in a small frying pan and pour in the egg mixture. Cook gently for about 2 minutes, then turn the omelette and cook for another minute. Set aside.

4 Brush your toastie maker with a little sunflower oil and switch on to pre-heat.

5 Place the cheese on one slice of bread. Add the ham, then the cooked omelette (folding it as necessary), along with the ketchup. Cover with the second slice of bread.

6 Close the lid of the toastie maker tightly and cook until the cheese melts and the bread is crispy and golden brown.

CHEFS NOTE

This recipe is based on Korean street food.

POSH TOASTIES

GRAPE AND BRIE TOASTIE

INGREDIENTS

- Sunflower oil for brushing
- Handful of red seedless grapes
- ½ avocado
- 2 slices seedy, wholegrain bread
- Wholegrain mustard
- 1 tbsp cream cheese
- A few slices Brie cheese
- Sea salt

METHOD

1 Brush your toastie maker with a little sunflower oil to help prevent sticking and make your toastie nice and crispy. Switch it on to pre-heat.

2 Meanwhile, wash the grapes and halve them. Peel, de-stone and slice the avocado.

3 Spread mustard on one piece of bread, cream cheese on the other. Cover the mustardy bread with slices of Brie, then arrange the grapes and avocado slices. Sprinkle with a little sea salt and cover with the other slice of bread, cream-cheese side down.

4 Transfer the sandwich to the toastie maker. Close the lid tightly and cook until the cheese melts and the bread is crispy and golden brown.

CHEFS NOTE

Grapes have been called the world's healthiest food. They're packed with antioxidants and nutrients.

CRANBERRY AND CAMEMBERT TOASTIE

INGREDIENTS

- 2 slices white bread
- Knob of butter
- 60g/2oz Camembert cheese
- 1 tbsp cranberry sauce
- 1 dash balsamic vinegar

METHOD

1 Switch on your toastie maker to pre-heat.

2 Meanwhile, butter the bread and slice the cheese.

3 Turn one slice of bread over and spread the Camembert evenly over the unbuttered side. Spread a thin layer of cranberry sauce over the cheese. Drizzle with a few drops of balsamic vinegar, and top with the remaining slice of bread, butter side up.

4 Transfer the sandwich to the heated toastie maker. Close the lid tightly and cook until the cheese melts and the bread is crispy and golden brown.

CHEFS NOTE

Brie makes a great substitute for Camembert.

BACON, BRIE AND GOAT'S CHEESE TOASTIE

INGREDIENTS

- 3 rashers bacon
- 50g/2oz Brie cheese
- 50g/2oz goat's cheese
- ½ tomato sliced
- Handful of watercress
- 2 slices bread
- Knob of butter
- Salt and freshly ground black pepper

METHOD

1 Grill the bacon until crisp. Break into pieces and set aside.

2 Switch on your toastie maker to pre-heat.

3 Meanwhile, slice the cheese. Rinse the tomato and watercress, and slice the tomato.

4 Butter the bread. Lay one slice, butter side down, in the toastie maker. Arrange the Brie slices on top, then the tomato, watercress, and goat's cheese. Top with the bacon pieces and season with salt and freshly ground black pepper. Cover with the remaining slice of bread, butter side up.

5 Close the lid of the toastie maker tightly and cook until the Brie melts and the bread is crispy and golden brown.

CHEFS NOTE

If you can't get goat's cheese, use mozzarella - though it isn't as posh!

POSH CHOCOLATE TOASTIE

INGREDIENTS

- 60ml/2floz evaporated milk
- 40g/1½oz dark chocolate, finely chopped
- Knob of butter
- 2 slices thin whole-wheat or white sandwich bread
- ½ tbsp dark or milk chocolate chips
- ½ tbsp chopped hazelnuts

METHOD

1 First, finely chop the dark chocolate. Heat the evaporated milk in a small pan until just boiling. Add the chocolate, let it stand for one minute, and then whisk until smooth. Let cool slightly.

2 Switch on your toastie maker to pre-heat.

3 Meanwhile, butter the bread. When the toastie machine is up to temperature, place one slice in it, butter side down. Spread the chocolate mixture over the bread, almost but not quite to the edges. Sprinkle on the chocolate chips and nuts. Cover with the remaining slice of bread, butter side up.

4 Close the lid of the toastie maker tightly and cook until the toast is golden and the chocolate barely melted.

CHEFS NOTE

Surprisingly, dark chocolate is actually good for you – it's probably the best source of antioxidants on the planet!

STEAK AND CREAM CHEESE TOASTIE

INGREDIENTS

- 50g/2oz steak
- 30g/1oz mushrooms, sliced
- ½ garlic clove
- 1 tbsp cream cheese
- Freshly ground black pepper
- 2 Slices of thick bread

METHOD

1 Grill or fry the steak as you like it, along with the sliced mushrooms.

2 Switch on your toastie maker to pre-heat.

3 Meanwhile, crush the garlic, and thinly slice the steak. Mix the cream cheese in a bowl with some black pepper and the garlic.

4 Butter the bread and place one slice, butter side down, in the toastie maker. Cover with the steak slices and mushrooms. Top with the cream cheese and cover with the remaining slice of bread, butter side up.

5 Close the lid of the toastie maker tightly and cook until the toast is crispy and golden brown.

CHEFS NOTE

If you don't have cream cheese, you can use a slice or two of hard cheese instead.

CREAMY CRAB TOASTIE

INGREDIENTS

- Sunflower oil for brushing
- 1 tomato
- 125g/4oz fresh crabmeat
- ½ tbsp mayonnaise
- ½ tbsp soured cream
- 2 spring onions
- Salt and freshly ground black pepper
- 2 slices bread
- 2 tbsp grated Parmesan cheese

METHOD

1 Rinse and slice the tomatoes & spring onions.

2 Brush your toastie maker with a little sunflower oil to help prevent sticking and make your toastie nice and crispy. Switch it on to pre-heat.

3 Meanwhile, in a medium bowl, gently mix the crabmeat, mayonnaise, soured cream and spring onions. Season with salt and pepper.

4 Place one slice of bread in the toastie maker. Arrange the slices of tomato on top, followed by the crabmeat mixture. Sprinkle the Parmesan cheese evenly over the top. Cover with the remaining slice of bread.

5 Close the lid of the toastie maker tightly and cook until the toast is crispy and golden brown.

CHEFS NOTE

Serve with a leafy green salad.

SMOKED SALMON AND CREAM CHEESE TOASTIE

INGREDIENTS

- 2 slices bread
- 2 tbsp soft full fat cheese
- 2-3 slices smoked salmon
- Handful fresh dill
- Lemon wedges and lemon juice

METHOD

1 Brush your toastie maker with a little sunflower oil to help prevent sticking and make your toastie nice and crispy. Switch it on to pre-heat.

2 Meanwhile, rinse and roughly chop the dill.

3 Lay one slice of bread in the heated toastie maker. Spread the soft cheese over it and season with salt and pepper. Arrange the salmon slices on top and sprinkle with the dill. Squeeze a dash of lemon juice over the top. Spread the remaining slice of bread with the rest of the soft cheese and place, cheesy side down, to close the sandwich.

4 Close the lid of the toastie maker tightly and cook until the toast is crispy and golden brown.

CHEFS NOTE

Smoked and unsmoked, salmon is one of the oily fish highest in omega 3 - serious brain food!

SWEET TOASTIES

CHOC, STRAWBERRY & BANANA TOASTIE

INGREDIENTS

- 2 slices bread
- Knob of butter
- 1 tbsp chocolate hazelnut spread
- 2 strawberries
- ½ banana

METHOD

- Switch on your toastie maker and bring up to temperature.
- Meanwhile, rinse the strawberries and remove the green tops. Peel and slice half a banana.
- Butter both slices of bread on one side, and cover the other sides in chocolate spread. Place one slice, butter side down, in the heated toastie maker. Layer on the slices of strawberry and banana, and close with the other slice of bread, butter side up.
- Close the lid tightly and cook until the bread is crispy and golden brown.

CHEFS NOTE

Strawberries are packed with vitamin C to help keep your brain focused.

WICKED SWEET TOASTIE

INGREDIENTS

- 2 slices of bread
- Knob of butter
- 1 chocolate bar of your choosing
- 1 handful marshmallows

METHOD

1 Switch on your toastie maker and bring it up to temperature.

2 Meanwhile, break the chocolate into squares or chunks. Butter the bread.

3 Place one slice of bread, butter side down, onto the heated toastie maker. Break up about 4-5 squares of chocolate onto the bread. Add a few marshmallows, but not so many that they'll spill out of the sandwich when it's shut in the machine. Top with the second slice of bread, butter side up.

4 Close the lid tightly and cook until the bread is crispy and golden brown.

CHEFS NOTE

Be careful as you lift it out, making sure not to get burned by drips of boiling chocolate or marshmallow.

SPICED BANANA & PEANUT BUTTER TOASTIE

INGREDIENTS

- 2 slices bread
- Knob of butter
- 2 tbsp crunchy peanut butter
- 1 banana
- ½ tsp ground cinnamon
- Pinch ground nutmeg
- Pinch all spice
- Pinch ground cloves

METHOD

1 Switch on your toastie maker and bring it up to temperature.

2 Meanwhile, butter the bread on one side and spread peanut butter on the other side of one of the pieces.

3 Place one slice of bread, butter side down, in the toastie maker. Peel the banana, cut it in half length-wise, and place it on top. Sprinkle on the cinnamon, nutmeg, all spice and cloves. Top with the second slice of bread, butter side up.

4 Close the lid tightly and cook until the bread is crispy and golden brown.

CHEFS NOTE

Peanut butter is high in protein and helps keep up your energy levels.

CHERRY CHEESECAKE TOASTIE

INGREDIENTS

- 2 slices bread
- Knob of butter
- 2 tbsp cream cheese
- 2 tbsp tinned cherry filling

METHOD

1 Switch on your toastie maker and bring it up to temperature.

2 Meanwhile, butter the bread on one side. When the machine is heated, place one slice in it, butter side down.

3 Layer on the cream cheese and cherry filling. Top with the second slice of bread, butter side up.

4 Close the lid tightly and cook until the bread is crispy and golden brown. Sprinkle with icing sugar and enjoy.

CHEFS NOTE

Try with brioche or other sweet bread.

PEANUT BUTTER, CHOC & BANANA TOASTIE

INGREDIENTS

- 2 slices bread
- Knob of butter
- 2 tbsp peanut butter
- ½ banana
- 3 squares of a chocolate bar
- Sprinkling of sugar

METHOD

1 Switch on your toastie maker and bring it up to temperature.

2 Butter the bread one side and spread peanut butter on the other. Break your chocolate bar into squares or chunks.

3 Place one slice of bread, butter side down, in the toastie maker. Add the chocolate. Peel and slice half a banana and add that. Top with the other slice of bread, butter side up.

4 Close the lid tightly and cook until the bread is crispy and golden brown. Sprinkle with icing sugar and enjoy.

CHEFS NOTE

You could use chocolate spread instead of a chocolate bar.

BLUEBERRY & CREAM CHEESE TOASTIE

INGREDIENTS

- 1 tbsp cream cheese
- 2 tsp icing sugar, plus more for dusting
- ½ tsp grated lemon zest
- 2 slices white bread
- Knob of butter
- 1 tbsp blueberry jam (or whatever jam you have)

METHOD

1 Grate a little zest from a fresh lemon.

2 Switch on your toastie maker and bring it up to temperature.

3 In a small bowl, mix the cream cheese, icing sugar and lemon zest.

4 Butter the bread on one side, and spread blueberry jam on the other.

5 Place one slice in the toastie maker, butter side down. Spoon the cheese mixture onto the centre, and top with the other slice of bread, butter side up.

6 Close the lid tightly and cook until the bread is crispy and golden brown. Sprinkle with a little more icing sugar and enjoy.

CHEFS NOTE

Delicious with a dollop of vanilla ice cream!

FRENCH STRAWBERRY TOASTIE

INGREDIENTS

- 4 strawberries
- A little sunflower oil for brushing
- 2 slices bread
- 1 tbsp cream cheese
- 1 egg
- Splash of milk
- Sprinkling of icing sugar

METHOD

1 Rinse the strawberries and remove the green tops before slicing them.

2 Brush your toastie maker with a little sunflower oil to help prevent sticking. Switch it on and bring up to temperature.

3 Meanwhile, whisk the egg in a bowl, with a splash of milk, then transfer to a shallow container.

4 Spread cream cheese on both sides of the bread. Make a sandwich with the sliced strawberries arranged between the bread slices. Then dip the whole sandwich into the egg mixture, so it's coated on both sides.

5 Place in the pre-heated toastie maker, close the lid tightly and cook until the bread is crispy and golden.

6 When they're ready, sprinkle them with icing sugar.

CHEFS NOTE

Sweet and nourishing, this toastie is food for comfort, brain and energy!

CREAM EGG TOASTIE

INGREDIENTS

- 2 slices bread
- Knob of butter
- 1 Cadbury cream egg

METHOD

1 Switch on your toastie maker and bring up to temperature.

2 Unwrap the cream egg and soften it in the microwave for a few seconds.

3 Butter the bread and place one slice, butter side down, in the pre-heated toastie maker. Break up the cream egg and squash it on to the bread. Add the other slice, butter side up.

4 Close the lid tightly and cook until the bread is crispy and golden brown.

CHEFS NOTE

Classic nutritious student food!!

BRIE AND HONEY TOASTIE

INGREDIENTS

- 2 slices bread
- Knob of butter
- 50g/2oz Brie cheese, sliced about half a centimetre thick
- 1 tbsp honey

METHOD

1 Switch on your toastie maker and bring up to temperature.

2 Meanwhile, cut enough slices of Brie to cover one bread slice. Butter the bread and lay one side in your pre-heated toastie maker.

3 Arrange the Brie slices on top, and add the honey. Cover with the remaining slice of bread, butter side up.

4 Close the lid tightly and cook until the bread is pale golden brown.

CHEFS NOTE

Honey helps the body absorb calcium and so can help boost memory and brain power as well as athletic performance.

APPLE, CINNAMON & RAISIN TOASTIE

INGREDIENTS

- Sunflower oil for brushing
- ½ apple
- 2 slices bread
- 1 tsp icing sugar
- Pinch ground cinnamon
- Small handful raisins

METHOD

1 Brush your toastie maker with a little sunflower oil to help prevent sticking and make your toastie nice and crispy. Switch it on to pre-heat.

2 Meanwhile, wash the apple, peel and core it and cut one half into thin slices. Arrange the apple over one slice of bread. Sprinkle icing sugar and a generous pinch of cinnamon over the top. Scatter over a few raisins then cover with the other slice of bread.

3 Transfer the sandwich to the toastie maker. Close the lid tightly and cook until the bread is crispy and golden brown.

CHEFS NOTE

Apples have a high vitamin C content, and help to focus the brain and keep you healthy.

BLACKBERRY & WHITE CHOCOLATE TOASTIE

INGREDIENTS

- 2 slices bread
- Knob of butter
- 1 large marshmallow
- 25g/1oz white chocolate, from a bar
- 4 ripe blackberries

METHOD

1 Switch on your toastie maker to pre-heat.

2 Rinse the blackberries, then lightly mash them with a fork to break them up. Break the chocolate into small pieces.

3 Butter the bread and lay one slice in the toastie machine, butter side down. Spread the squashed blackberries on the bread, then scatter the chocolate pieces and add the marshmallow in the middle. Squash it down with the other slice of bread, butter side up.

4 Close the lid of the toastie maker tightly and cook until the bread is crispy and golden brown.

CHEFS NOTE

Recent studies have shown blackberries to be good for brain health.

TOASTIE EXTRAS

CHILLI JAM

Makes 4 jam jars

INGREDIENTS

- 4 red peppers
- 8 red chillies
- 6 garlic cloves
- 750g/1lb 11oz sugar
- 500ml/2 cups red wine vinegar
- 4 sterilised jam jars

METHOD

1 Deseed the peppers, cut the stalks off the chillies (don't bother deseeding them) and peel the garlic cloves.

2 Place these into a food processor and pulse until finely chopped.

3 Add this, along with the sugar and red wine vinegar into a non-stick saucepan.

4 Bring to the boil and leave to gently simmer for about 50-60mins without stirring. After this time the liquid should be a little thicker and more jam like. Cook for a further 10-15 minutes stirring occasionally.

5 Leave to settle for 10 minutes. Divide into sterilised jars, close the lids and leave to cool completely. Should store for at least 8 weeks, refrigerate once opened.

CHEFS NOTE

Adjust the amount of chillies to suit your own taste.

OLIVE TAPENADE

Enough For 4-6 Toasties

INGREDIENTS

- 200g/7oz pitted kalamata olives
- 4 tbsp extra virgin olive oil
- Large bunch of flat leaf parsley
- 3 tbsp capers
- 2 garlic cloves
- Salt & pepper

METHOD

1 Place the olives, oil, parsley, capers & garlic in a food processor and blitz until finely chopped.

2 Season with salt & pepper and store in the fridge for up to 3 days.

CHEFS NOTE

Try adding a twist of lemon juice for a fresher flavour or some anchovy fillets for a deeper flavour.

HOMEMADE PESTO

INGREDIENTS

- Large bunch of basil
- 100g/3½oz pine nuts
- 100g/3 ½oz grated Parmesan cheese
- 380ml/1½ cups olive oil
- 2 garlic cloves
- Salt & pepper

METHOD

1 Place the basil, pine nuts, cheese, olive oil & garlic in a food processor with plenty of salt and pepper. Pulse until you have a smooth pesto paste.

2 Adjust the seasoning, add a little more oil if needed and store in the fridge for up to 5 days.

CHEFS NOTE

Feel free to alter the balance of garlic, cheese and salt to suit your own taste.

BEETROOT CHUTNEY

INGREDIENTS

- 200g/7oz cooked beetroot
- ½ red onion, peeled
- 2 tbsp balsamic vinegar
- 2 tbsp olive oil
- 1 tbsp orange juice
- Salt & pepper

METHOD

1 Place the beetroot, onion, vinegar & oil in a food processor and blitz until finely chopped.

2 Season with salt & pepper and store in the fridge for up to 3 days.

CHEFS NOTE

Use vacuum packed, fresh cooked beetroot for this simple no-cook chutney.

HUMMOUS

INGREDIENTS

- 200g/7oz tinned chickpeas, drained
- 2 tbsp Greek yoghurt
- 2 garlic cloves
- 6 tbsp olive oil
- 1 tbsp lemon juice
- 2 tbsp tahini paste
- 1 tsp ground cumin
- ½ tsp sea salt

METHOD

1 Place the chickpeas, yoghurt, garlic, oil, lemon juice, tahini paste & cumin in a food processor and blitz until you have a smooth paste.

2 Adjust the garlic, lemon and tahini to suit your own taste. Check the seasoning and store in the fridge for up to 3 days.

CHEFS NOTE

The Greek yoghurt gives this hummous a rich creaminess.

GUACAMOLE

Enough For 4-6 Toasties

INGREDIENTS

- 2 avocados, peeled & stoned
- 1 garlic clove, crushed
- 3 tbsp lime juice
- 1 tsp paprika
- Large bunch of fresh coriander, finely chopped

METHOD

1 Cut the avocado flesh into cubes and combine this with the garlic, lime juice, paprika & chopped coriander.

2 Use the back of a fork to crush some, but not all, of the avocado cubes (so that you are left with a chunky guacamole).

3 Season with salt & pepper and store in the fridge for up to 3 days.

CHEFS NOTE

You could blitz this in a food processor if you prefer a smoother texture.

ROASTED PEPPERS

Enough For 4-6 Toasties

INGREDIENTS

- 6 red peppers, deseeded & halved
- 3 garlic cloves, crushed
- 2 tbsp olive oil
- 1 tsp dried rosemary
- ½ tsp sea salt

METHOD

1 Preheat the oven to 180C/350F/Gas 4

2 Place the peppers, garlic, oil, rosemary & salt in a bowl and combine well to coat each pepper piece in the herby oil.

3 Lay the peppers out on a baking tray and cook in the preheated oven for approx. 30 minutes or until the peppers are deliciously roasted and cooked through.

4 Leave to cool. Cover and store in the fridge for up to 3 days.

CHEFS NOTE

Yellow or orange peppers are also fine to use, but avoid the more bitter tasting green peppers.

SIMPLE HOMEMADE COLESLAW

Enough For 4-6 Toasties

INGREDIENTS

- ½ green pointed cabbage
- 2 carrots, peeled & topped
- 2-3 tsp Dijon mustard
- 3 tbsp mayonnaise
- 4 spring onions

METHOD

1 You can either grate/shred the cabbage and carrots before combining with all the other ingredients in a bowl, or alternatively place everything in a food processor and pulse until chopped to the right consistency.

2 Season with salt & pepper and store in the fridge for up to 3 days.

CHEFS NOTE

Fresh and crunchy, you can serve this coleslaw with any of the savoury toasties in this book.

OTHER COOKNATION TITLES

If you enjoyed I Love My Sandwich Toaster *you may also like other titles in the* **I♥MY** *series.*

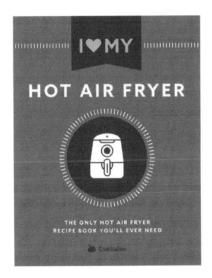

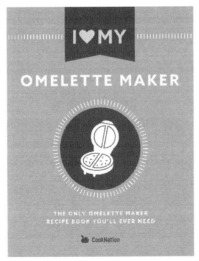

To browse the full catalogue visit
www.bellmackenzie.com

Printed in Great Britain
by Amazon